ADVENTURES *in* home staging

Practical advice to help transform your home from so-so to

SOLD!

By Patti A. Pierucci
R EALTOR®, Professional Home Stager

*For Betty,
It was so great to meet you… looking forward to helping you find your new home.
Patti*

Adventures in Home Staging:

*Practical Advice to Help
Transform Your Home from So-So to SOLD*

By Patti A. Pierucci
© 2016 by Pierucci, Inc.

ISBN-13:
978-0692993200 (Pierucci, Inc.)

ISBN-10:
0692993207

TABLE OF CONTENTS

Introduction..1

Chapter 1: Red Rocks..6

Chapter 2: Declutter..12

Chapter 3: Spot Remover...15

Chapter 4: Directions Included...20

Chapter 5: Clean, then Clean Again.....................................22

Chapter 6: Get to the Point..28

Chapter 7: Listen to Your REALTOR® and Paint.................31

Chapter 8: Home Buyer, Thy name is Woman...................33

Chapter 9: Grab Them at the Curb.......................................37

Chapter 10: No Vacancy...40

Chapter 11: I Did What?..44

Conclusion...48

Summary of Tips..50

Acknowledgements..52

INTRODUCTION

After a particularly exhausting day of home staging, conducted at the home of a widower gentleman with a yearning to return to his family in England, I completed rearranging the master suite and left him with these instructions:

"Be sure to make your bed every day, just like I have made it here. Stand the pillows up at a 90-degree angle, pillows in the back, shams in front of those, then the throw pillows arranged exactly like this in the front. Got it?"

This gentleman, with his charming British accent and wicked sense of humor, wryly asked if I could draw him a diagram. We laughed and left for home, sleeping off the day's work in preparation for another day of real estate sales, listings and possibly more Home Staging.

The next morning I thought of this widower, who had lost his wife just one year earlier, and had survived a day of our team's energetic Staging. I called him and asked how he was adjusting to all the changes in his home.

"Well," he began, accent charming as ever, "I didn't think I'd remember the instructions for the bed pillows, and I didn't want to mess up the bed because I knew I'd never get it back the way you made it, so I just slept at the bottom of the made-up bed all night."

He added that he intended to do the same thing every night until the house sold.

Whether or not this admission was one of his many jokes I never knew, but every time I stopped at his house the master bed was impeccably made.

This story underscores one of the important things about Home Staging: Home Staging involves a change in lifestyle for many home owners, sometimes an uncomfortable change. But change that prepares the home to sell is vitally important in the new world of real estate in which we live.

Why another book on Home Staging? Most REALTORS® and sellers already know that they need to declutter and clean up to sell a home, right?

WRONG! The vast majority of homes that I show resemble some of the worst aspects of my own home, which is well lived in, only occasionally picked up or ready for company, and with a lot of STUFF all over the place.

This is the way most people live, because our homes are not showplaces for other people to admire; they are our comfort zones … our havens with soft, well-worn pillows … sometimes hairy pets that snuggle up with us on the lumpy but comfortable sofa … furniture that is arranged around a giant-screen TV for maximum viewing pleasure, even if it blocks the entrance to the kitchen … and bright blue walls that match the plaid in the huge recliner that Uncle Joe lives in nearly 24 hours a day.

But living in a home day to day is not the same as preparing it for sale. That's where Home Staging comes in. Where once sellers and their agents used common sense to set the stage for a sale by painting walls a neutral beige or white, removing clutter and cleaning the house, today it has become a much more complex endeavor. It is, in fact, a major industry.

Following the bubble in the mid-2000s, when prices suddenly stopped their meteoric rise and began to plummet, and when sales that had been off the charts began to slow to a trickle in nearly every housing market in the nation, REALTORS® began to realize the

With my Staging partner and Broker, Judy Woten.

necessity of making their listings more appealing than everything else on the market. In a strong buyers' market, the two important ways to win the sale are to price it right — and Stage it.

The concept of Staging has been around for decades, but it became a sort of art form in the mid- to late-2000s, and it is now a multi-million-dollar industry. Home Stagers with all kinds of credentials, accreditations and experience are making their mark in the real estate industry by helping agents and their sellers to put the best faces possible on their homes.

I conduct my Home Staging with my Staging partner and Broker, Judy Woten. We received accreditation through the Association of Staging Professionals (ASP) nearly a decade ago, and we have accumulated rooms full of Staging items that we alternately haul in and out of homes to help them sell.

So, does it work? ABSOLUTELY!

My own experiences bear it out, but more important is that the statistics don't lie. A 2015 study of Home Staging conducted by the National Association of REALTORS® revealed the following:

- Among REALTORS® who typically represent the buyer, 49 percent reported most buyers are affected by Home Staging.
- Buyers report that a Staged home makes it easier for them to visualize the property as a future home (81 percent).

REALTORS® Represent Buyer Side

Most likely to be impacted by viewing a staged home:

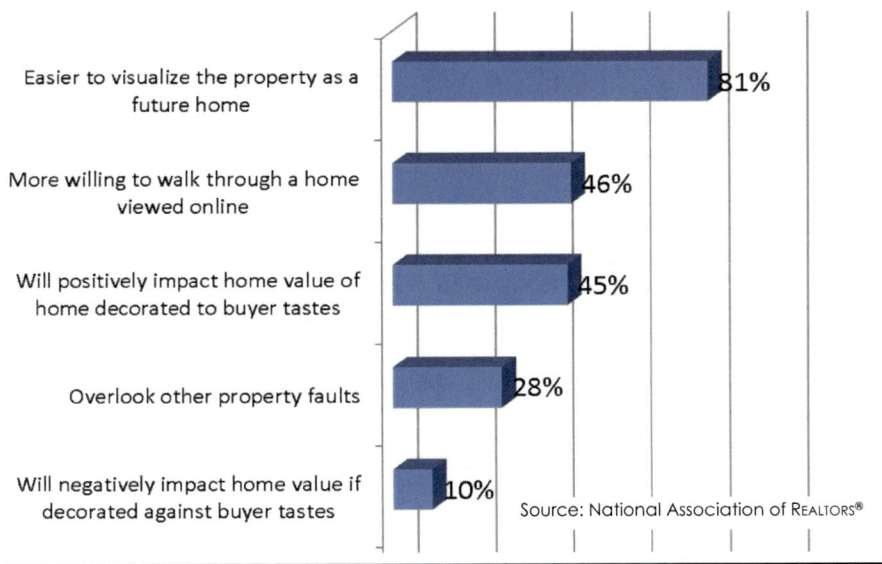

Source: National Association of REALTORS®

- Buyers are more willing to overlook other property faults (28 percent) in Staged homes.

- Most important, a whopping 81 percent of buyers find a Staged home easier to visualize as their future home. **That number alone is reason enough to Stage.**

So to home owners who may be thinking of selling their homes — as well as real estate agents who don't know how to sell that cluttered mess of a home, this book is for you. These are my best tips, gleaned from years of experience tackling some of the most difficult

Staging assignments imaginable. If I and my Staging partner, Judy, can take on these challenges and get them sold ...

... so can you!

Chapter 1
Red Rocks

A few years ago I received a referral from a client whose home I had Staged and sold. The referral welcomed me into her home when I arrived with my crew and boxes of Staging items. When I began to pull out my red accent pieces — red pillows, red plates and cups, red vases and red flowers — she laughed.

"My friend warned me that you would do the 'red' thing," said my seller. So we did our red thing, took the photos for the listing, put it on the market, and the home sold in a few weeks. The "red thing" really works.

Color fads come and go. Today — at least in our Lynchburg, Virginia, regional market — gray is the new beige. Cool colors are in, warm colors are out. Gray and coastal blues have replaced REALTOR® beige as the new "it" color for walls. In many markets, the hot new decorating scheme is coastal, with its pastel-hued shades of turquoise, blue and coral. But my Staging partner and I often continue to fall back on red because, well ... red really rocks it when it comes to providing a bold pop of color ... and it looks great in listing photos.

Evidence that RED ROCKS. On the right, the red curtains and other small pops of red pull the eye around this room and evoke a feeling of comfort and space. At left, in the before photo, the same room with more furniture looks crowded, disorganized and uncomfortable.

Research bears this out. Not only is red a bright, eye-catching color but it actually causes a physical reaction in people: It increases the heart rate, breathing rate and blood pressure. The color red also inspires feelings of "excitement and passion." Retailers have long known this and have used red to generate enthusiasm for a product.

The color red also shows up beautifully in photos. The main goal of Home Staging is to tell the viewer what to look at in a room, and to draw the eye to certain features. Using a red accent, be it a curtain panel or valence, a pillow or bouquet of flowers, immediately draws the eye to the greenery outside the window, the sofa placement, and the dining room in which the flowers are sitting.

And in doing so the red also draws the eye AWAY from features that you don't want the viewer to linger on — such as the small room size, or the low ceiling, the old-fashioned linoleum flooring, etc.

TIP #1: Use color strategically to draw the eye around a room and away from features you don't want to highlight.

Of course, many other colors are functional and appealing when Staging a home:

Blue is a calming color that puts buyers at ease and makes them feel comfortable. Blue is known to inspire feelings of loyalty and trustworthiness in viewers. But a too-bright blue, especially on the walls, is a no-no. In fact, any color placed on a wall that is too bold is going to turn off buyers and make the room look smaller — and that most definitely includes red.

Another great staging color is orange. Traditionally orange is attractive because it offers something different to the viewer. More and more it is being used by decorators, and Home Stagers are no different in realizing its value as an accent color. Used sparingly, it

Orange accents can be quite stunning, but should be used sparingly and with colors that are complementary, such as blues and greens.

can modernize and provide some spunk to an otherwise old-fashioned room.

Green commonly makes viewers think of money. It's a favorite color choice for financial institutions because it implies wealth, success and growth — but it should be used with care in Home Staging. Deep or bright green colors should be avoided, unless used in simple pops of color. More soothing greens like moss green, seafoam green and even lime green can be quite appealing as accents and even as wall colors.

Color Coordinating

Many people, including REALTORS®, buyers and sellers, may know instinctively what colors go with others. But sometimes the pairings can be jarring to the eye if you don't get them right.

For instance, if you're using red as an accent, don't pair it with deep blue or you will conjure images of the American flag and patriotism. While there's obviously nothing wrong with symbols of America, they are not appealing as a home color scheme.

So when using red as an accent in a room, pair it with warm beiges, browns, subtle greens and light blues (don't go too Christmas with the reds and greens), yellows and oranges.

The color wheel on the next page is a good guide. It can help you match and combine colors. The basic primary colors are red, yellow and blue, in the center of wheel — which are used to create all the secondary colors like purple, aqua and orange. Tertiary colors, or third-level colors, are created by mixing primary and secondary colors together, in the outer circle.

What's more, there are warm colors and cool colors. Warm colors include orange, red, yellow and some yellow-greens. Cool colors include blue, green and purple.

A good general rule to follow — although it can be broken in subtle

A typical color wheel shows the relationships between primary colors, secondary colors and tertiary (third level) colors (which are created by mixing primary and secondary colors). Analogous colors are colors next to each other on the wheel. For example, yellow and green. Complementary colors are colors across from each other on a color wheel. For example, blue and orange. Triadic colors, which are groups of three colors, are colors that are evenly across from each other, in a triangle over the color wheel. For example, the primary colors red, yellow, and blue are triadic colors.

ways — is to mix warm colors with warm colors and cool colors with cool colors.

If you look at the color wheel you can often pair a color with its opposite on the wheel, which is its complementary color. For instance, orange and blue go great together, but when Staging don't overdo it. Try to pick one color as your primary accent color, then weave in some other colors that are complementary in smaller ways.

Remember: These so-called rules are really just guidelines. They're made to be broken, or at the least bent. If it looks good, and you're-combining colors in strategic or subdued ways, go for it. If you're not sure how buyers will perceive it, take a picture and see how it looks on your computer screen.

Photos, usually first seen online, are king when it comes to Staging — and when it comes to selling a home. The vast majority, more than 90 percent, of all buyers begin their home searches online, according to the National Association of REALTORS®.

Whether you are a REALTOR® or selling your home yourself (which is a very bad idea, but that's another book), by all means hire a professional photographer!

> **TIP #2: ALWAYS consider how the room you are Staging will look in a photo. If the valence you're placing on the window is drawing the eye to a broken window pane, re-think the valence.**

One of my colleagues, Steve Burkett, takes all of my photos. He's got the professional equipment and lighting to do our photos justice. Don't rely on your iphone to give you professional quality photos for your listing. In the long run it will be money well spent.

If the photos don't grab the buyer, or if the colors look too bold, or too soft, then the buyer may move on to a home that could be worse looking than yours in person, but may just have more inviting photos on display.

If you don't have photos posted online at all, you've just lost a prospective buyer.

Chapter 2
Declutter

Studies show that most people move to a new home because they need more space for their stuff. So one of the first and most important rules in Home Staging is: Declutter.

If your home is filled with collectibles, pictures on every wall, stuff not put away, then buyers will get the impression your home doesn't have enough space for them.

Decluttering can mean different things to different people, but to put it in Staging terms, it means to remove items from your rooms that are not helping its appeal.

One rule I've adopted is that small items, even if there are just two or three of them in a room, will look like clutter in a picture. Tiny things simple don't show up as anything at all in photos, and remember that photos are king when it comes to listing your home.

But if two or three tiny objects are clutter, imagine what a glass-doored curio cabinet filled with 200 tiny things will look like in a photo — not to mention to the buyer who will not be able to pass it

The sellers of this house agreed to declutter thier kitchen and modernize it by replacing the dated appliances, left, with stainless steel appliances, right. In addition to removing the table and most of the countertop items, this kitchen looked bigger and more modern, and the home was under contract in just four days.

The multiple tiny tchotchkes (knick-nacks) in the kitchen on the left may look great up close, but they end up looking like clutter in the photo. Removing most of them, including the items on the refrigerator, makes the room look less hectic and larger.

by without stopping to stare at it.

Clutter creates confusion to the eye, which creates confusion in the brain. The buyer of a home needs to see the focal point first, then have his/her eye swept around the room by carefully crafted Staging techniques that control where the eye goes. The last thing you want your home decor to do is to stop this flow.

Some collections can be breathtakingly beautiful. I recall showing one home that contained the most beautiful hand-made quilt hangings I had ever seen. The owner was a professional quilter and her home was a great backdrop for her talent.

But you couldn't walk through the home without stopping at one of the quilts and admiring its intricate details, the stories that they told, and the themes they represented. But if I had been a buyer I would have been slowed to a crawl in this house, and would never have appreciated the "big picture" — the spacious rooms, the large stone fireplace, the wall-to-wall windows in the great room, and more. The collection of quilts was getting in the way of my appreciation of the home's other features.

On the flip side, some collections can be so taste-specific they deserve some mention. Do NOT show off your collection of deer heads (covered more fully in the next chapter). And do not show off your collection of nude paintings (what may be art to one person could be pornography to another). Some people love Hummel figurines, some do not. Use common sense and restraint in displaying any collectibles.

> **TIP #3: Declutter every room, closet and space in your house by removing items that don't enhance its appeal.**

Some tips for decluttering:

- Remove or thin out displays of collectibles, such as china cabinets, curios, dolls, sports-themed collections, etc.
- Remove tiny objects throughout the house that won't show well in photos.
- Remove most items, except those that you use every day, from kitchen and bathroom countertops.
- Declutter closets by packing up clothes that are unused or out of season and store them away. Neatly hang up clothes.
- Declutter bathroom vanities of all personal toiletry items by storing in a basket and stowing beneath the sink for easy access.
- Declutter children's rooms by putting toys away in toy chests or closets.
- Leave the corners of rooms as open as possible. This visually tricks the eye into seeing a more spacious room.

> **TIP #4: Leave the corners of rooms as open as possible to create the impression of more space.**

Chapter 3

Spot Remover

My Staging partner, Judy, and I have walked into many homes that immediately transported us to other places. Sometimes we're transported to another galaxy in kids' bedrooms that are covered with glow-in-the-dark ceiling stars, or Star Trek-themed bedding.

One former client, a single man with a large property and log cabin home, decorated the entire house in camouflage. The master suite bed was covered in a Mossy Oak-patterned quilt; the bathroom had a camouflage shower curtain and khaki green towels; the living room was like a wildlife get-together with nearly every wall covered

The only buyer this room is likely to appeal to is a hunter. Even the average male will find this woodsy, earthy, camo-festooned design too off-putting. Staging your home to appeal to this limited buying demographic violates the rules laid out in Chapter 7: Appeal to the women, who make most of the home-buying decisions in the United States.

with deer heads, antlers and animal skins. And to top it all off, the kitchen curtains sported the same camo motif as all the other rooms.

He simply would not consider removing the camo décor, and his cabin never sold.

Another seller eagerly welcomed us into her home one day for us to create a Staging plan. With chagrin we noticed that every bedroom had an animal-skin theme. One room was covered with zebra stripes, from the black and white lampshade to the dizzying pattern on the bedspread. Another room was covered in leopard spots. Another bedroom was decorated in a pony theme.

By all means, decorate your home in whatever colors, themes and patterns you want. But when you're selling, get out the spot remover and neutralize your home.

TIP #5: Neutralize strong themes in rooms to appeal to the largest number of buyers.

In another house we Staged, a creative homeowner turned a downstairs bedroom into a beach scene, with flip-flops and beach towels decorating the walls. Only the sand was missing. It was actually quite fun — but too fun and quirky to appeal to a broad pool of buyers.

I recently read about a $1.26 million home on the market in Texas that included a room with a full Star Trek theme built into it. The media room had a recreation of the bridge of the Star Trek USS Enterprise, complete with a cinema screen. It also included spaceship-inspired bunk beds, a "Trekkie" kitchen and dining room, outer space ceilings, and a futuristic bathroom.

Unless you're a Trekkie — and I'm not judging here — you're going to have the same reaction I did when I saw the pictures: "How much will it cost to tear out all that Star Trek design and turn the room into a normal bedroom?" That's exactly the same thought a buyer would have.

All of these scenarios are Staging nightmares, but they serve as perfect, though extreme, examples of what not to do. Don't allow your favorite sports team, camo pattern, movie, fabric pattern, or any other location on earth to dominate your Staging décor.

If you have more than one leopard or tiger print in the room, you've got at least one too many.

Here's another tip: If you arrive at a house like the Star Trek-themed one to do Home Staging, and if the owner greets you at the door with fake Vulcan ears and gives you the "live long and prosper" hand greeting, you know immediately you're about to go boldly where few Home Stagers have ever gone.

TIP #6: Be respectful of sellers' belongings, and of their strong connection to their home's decor.

Few of us live in a Staged home (except for my Staging partner Judy, who has zero tolerance for clutter and dirt generated by husbands, kids and pets), yet to sell a home and set the stage for a buyer we must convince sellers to go through this grueling process.

For some sellers, it's a piece of cake. They live in Spartan houses with very little clutter or junk lying about. But these are rare birds, indeed, because most people sell their homes precisely because their stuff has outgrown their space, and they need to move into bigger homes that will accommodate their stuff.

If I were to place my own home on the market, I would need several weeks to declutter, clean, paint, re-arrange furniture ... and have a strong talking-to with my husband and dog about keeping the house neat.

Speaking of my husband, when we fixed up his house in order to sell it, it was my first experience with the deep emotional connection that many sellers have to their homes. My husband kept running across little plastic toys that his children had played with and discarded decades ago.

"Save this," he would say handing me a grimy doll's head with one eye missing. "Cindy (his daughter) may want this."

I knew that Cindy would NEVER want that old dismembered doll's head, but I didn't say that to my husband. And to this day I try to remind myself of this incident when I am barking out instructions to home sellers like a drill sergeant. Yes, I've always been great at throwing stuff away, but not everyone is as ruthless as I am.

As REALTORS® we must understand how difficult the process can be for sellers. It is not easy to get rid of your stuff. But for those sellers

The theme of this kitchen seemed to be, "Let's party!" But it was overwhelming the space and making this well-appointed kitchen look shabby. By decluttering and removing many of the items, including the plethora of refrigerator magnets and notes, the buyer can now see the kitchen's full potential. What's more, you can now see that this kitchen offers granite countertops and loads of cabinet space.

Competing patterns and colors, above, plus a big lounge chair right in front of the entryway, made this room hard to appreciate. Rugs can be helpful in Staging, but don't have to be used at all when the floors are a selling feature. A modest amount of decluttering, opening up the corners, and bringing our "red rocks" strategy into play helped sell this house in four days!

---

who are very resistant and may be reading this, remember: You are NOT selling your home, you're selling a house; you're selling square footage. If you keep that in mind, you'll understand the importance of setting a proper stage to showcase your square footage.

> **TIP #7: You're not selling your home; you're selling square footage.**

Chapter 4

Directions Included

I've often said that more women should become builders and architects because we're the ones who usually have to decorate the rooms. And let's face it, some homes are downright quirky.

I listed a split-level home in Lynchburg, Virginia, that had four levels, and only three of them had obvious purposes. Once we got down to level four, which was below the first basement level, we were out of Staging options. *What are we supposed to Stage this room for?* we wondered.

Part of it had been a one-car basement carport, which was finished off, carpeted and blended into another small room that contained a half bathroom. It was being used as a catch-all for the owners' belongings. Odd pieces of furniture, storage boxes, lounge chairs and more were all competing for attention.

We decided to clear out the clutter and create an office space in this oddball room, *and the home sold in just four days.*

There are some room themes that are exceptions to the general rule that says do NOT create a theme in your room, discussed in the last chapter. One is the home office. If you have a bedroom to spare, by all means Stage it as a home office. Since nearly everyone has a computer today and needs a place to use it at home, the Staged home office can be a great theme room to help sell a home.

Just resist the urge to add another theme on top of the home office — such as using it as a display case for your guns, deer heads, baseball paraphernalia ... or Star Trek memorabilia. Collections are fine to display, but be conservative and thoughtful about it.

This space worked perfectly for the homeowner, but not for the prospective buyer who could not *feel* how the space could be used. We added lighting to the fireplace to highlight this previously hidden gem, then we re-oriented the sitting space around the fireplace. If it had been in the budget, the TV could have been wired and mounted into the top of the fireplace, but by keeping it angled in the corner it allowed the buyer to notice the room's primary feature: The fireplace.

In the case of this converted carport in the four-level split home, the quirky fourth level worked perfectly as an office, and it showed buyers how the room could be used.

We frequently Stage basement rooms as TV retreat rooms, with a big bowl of popcorn and comfy pillows strewn about.

TIP #8: Most buyers need to be shown the room's purpose. Show buyers how to use the room by Staging it.

Another way to Stage an odd space anywhere in the house is to transform it into a game room, or game area of a room. Place a small table in the space with an open game board on top, and buyers can picture themselves or their families enjoying the space.

A small extra room can also be Staged as a craft room. But left unstaged or vacant it can prompt buyers to scratch their heads and ask, "What am I supposed to do with this tiny room?" Make sure you answer that question for them before it's even asked.

Keep this in mind: Most buyers can't imagine how the room should be used. Staging can help give them the directions they need to understand how to use the room. A sale in four days flat could be the reward for your Staging efforts.

Chapter 5
Clean, Then Clean Again

When my Staging partner, Judy Woten, and I walked into a ranch home in Lynchburg one day to Stage it, we began to unpack our boxes and bags of bedspreads and kitchen nicknacks.

Pretty quickly I felt a bug bite on my arm and swatted it away. Almost simultaneously I noticed Judy swatting away her own insect. Within a few minutes we were both scratching and swatting hundreds of tiny hopping, blood-sucking insects — fleas. The home was infested with fleas!

In this instance we were unable to finish our Staging, so bad was the infestation. By the time we hurriedly packed up our items and scurried out of the house, we were covered with bug bites.

This home had an unusual level of dirtiness that we rarely see in homes. Try to imagine a couple of buyers walking into the home and suddenly having their ankles attacked by these horrid bloodsuckers before they can reach the kitchen.

Needless to say, this home was destined to sit on the market, and no amount of Home Staging could save it. This brings me to …

TIP #9: There is no substitute for a clean house. Clean sells!

ANYBODY can have a dirty, disheveled house, so if that's all you're offering, just keep it off the market and stay where you are — because buyers want a house that screams: "I'm different from your house!" And a clean, tidy home is the best way to convey that message.

When I first began my real estate career I recall showing a home that I have never been able to erase from my memory. As soon as I entered with my buyer, the smells assaulted us. Then the piles of unwashed clothing assaulted us, one pile topped off with dirty underwear sitting like a cherry on top of a melting ice cream sundae.

This house was a mess from front to back. The walls were covered with grime; the kitchen counters were not even visible beneath the piles of dirty dishes and clutter. The bedrooms seemed to be as small as closets because of all the clothes piled up. How many clothes could one family accumulate?

My buyer could not escape fast enough, and neither could I. It didn't matter that this home was the right price, the right size, in the right location for my buyer. This filthy eyesore was going to be someone else's new home, NOT my buyer's.

Another listing of mine was an odorous one from the beginning. After repainting every square inch, then cleaning from top to bottom, the odor still lingered in the carpeting. My client simply could not smell it, and he insisted on listing the home.

The first two prospective buyers through the door were appalled at the smell and passed on the house. With this evidence in hand, I convinced the home owner to replace the carpeting and the smell magically disappeared as the truck drove away, carrying with it the stinky old carpeting.

Clean your home as if your life depends on it — because in a way, it does. Your new life in a new home will only happen if you can sell your existing home, so clean, clean, clean … then clean it again!

For the cleaning challenged, here's a list of how to approach the job of cleaning your house:

Kitchen:

- Vacuum, mop and, if needed, wax the floors.
- Vacuum and then mop your linoleum or your vinyl floors.
- Wash and clean the baseboards.
- Clean the inside and the outside of the refrigerator — yes, clean the inside, too!
- Change the shelf liners. If you don't have shelf liners, lay them down — then clean them!
- Clean and organize the kitchen junk drawer.
- Wipe inside and outside of the cabinets.

Bathroom:

- Scrub the toilet from top to bottom.
- Scrub sinks, faucets and hardware.
- Wipe off drawers and vanity attachments.
- Clean the floors.
- Clean the mirrors.
- Organize the linen closet, remove unused linen to create the impression of more space.

Windows:

- Wash the windows.
- Dust the windowsills.
- Clean window tracks
- Clean the window screens
- Vacuum or dust the draperies.
- Clean the blinds.

Furniture:

- Polish the wood furniture.
- Vacuum cloth upholstery. Clean and condition leather upholstery on furniture.
- Vacuum under and in between cushions.
- Clean under the sofas. Yes, buyers may actually look beneath your furniture!

The owner of this home was the mother of a rambunctious toddler and a newborn, not to mention four dogs — so she had her hands full keeping *anything* in the house clean, let alone the kitchen. But by simply cleaning away the clutter (clutter for most people is stuff they use every day!), buyers can see the countertop space, and they can see more of the new stainless steel appliances.

Closets:

- Donate clothing you no longer use to charity or bring it to a consignment shop. Pack up and remove out-of-season clothing for your new home.

- Vacuum the floors.

- Dust the walls and the shelves.

- Place cedar blocks in the closet to freshen the air and prevent moths.

- Paint the inside of your closet if needed.

Cleaning Baseboards:

- Grab a clean, absorbent rag and dampen it in a soapy solution, wringing it as dry as possible.

- Start at one end of the baseboard and wipe all the way along the top and the sides. Go around the room.

- By the time you finish, the cleaned baseboard should be dry.

- Go over the baseboards again with a used fabric softener tissue from your dryer. This will help prevent dust from settling on the clean baseboard.

Carpet Cleaning:

- Sprinkle baking soda on your carpets to absorb stale or musty odors. Vacuum after one hour. If needed, have your carpets professionally cleaned. If that doesn't work, install new carpeting!

TIP #10: Eliminate all odors from the house with a thorough house cleaning. Don't try to mask strong odors with a lot of plug-ins, perfumes or candles.

Chapter 6

Get to the Point

You've probably heard it said that every room needs a focal point, but all too often the rooms in which we live have several focal points. For instance, what about the master bedroom that includes a bed, a seating area, a large-screen TV and a computer desk? What's the focal point in that room?

The answer is: The bed. And if you walk into that room and don't immediately get a feel for how you can get a comfortable night's sleep, then the room needs to be Staged. You may need to remove the computer or, heaven forbid, the TV, so that buyers can "feel" that it is a bedroom.

Rooms can have multiple purposes, like the master bedroom described above, but it should — with a few exceptions — have only one main focal point of interest.

The focal point is the thing you see immediately when you walk into the room. Often the focal point is only a starting point for your eyes, which may be drawn to the focal point (if the Staging is ac-

We created an additional sitting area in this awkward space by removing some unnecessary furniture and decluttering. When a large space presents a Staging dilemma, consider dividing it up and creating multiple uses.

complishing its purpose), and then are carried around the room to the sofa, the TV, the rocking chair and the bookshelf — creating a sense of space and flow for the buyer's eye.

This is the essence of Home Staging, to immediately snap the buyer's eye to the focal point, then drag the eye around the room to create an sense of space and comfort.

Focal points for various rooms may be:

- The fireplace in a living room.
- The island decorated with place settings in the kitchen.
- The granite countertops in the kitchen.
- The king-size bed in the master suite.
- The TV in the recreation room.
- The table in the dining room.
- The desk in the office.

The concept may seem simple, but in practice it can be a difficult fit for many sellers' lifestyles. One young mother with two active toddlers explained to me why her living room consisted of one chair and a round maze of plastic fencing which surrounded a thick plastic floor pad and dozens of toys. Inside the fence maze were her two little boys,

"There was an old woman who lived in a shoe, thanks to an award-winning realtor who was able to meet her unusual and eccentric needs."

who ran, fell, cried and bounced against the fence like balls in a pinball machine.

"There's no way I can keep furniture in this room," said the harried mother. "My boys are just too destructive."

Unfortunately for this mother, she was hurting her chances of a sale by not Staging a living room for buyers to view. Her living room looked like a pepperoni pizza in the photos, one of the fastest ways to scare off a buyer. It doesn't hurt to repeat TIP#8 here:

TIP #8: Most buyers need to be shown the room's purpose. Show buyers how to use the room by Staging it.

The view above left was what would have greeted the buyer upon walking into the house if we had not Staged it. At right, it's obvious that some rearranging of furniture and decluttering made the rooms look larger, and also gave them a purpose. What's more, you can now see the focal point of the living room: the gaslog fireplace, not to mention the beautiful floors and beyond that ... the outdoors.

Chapter 7
Listen to Your REALTOR® and PAINT!

One of the first requests your REALTOR® is likely to make is, please re-paint your house. "But it really doesn't need it," may be the home owner's response. "Paint anyway," says your REALTOR®, "and don't forget to paint the trim, as well."

This chapter is just a quick reminder that painting your home is the cheapest, easiest way to gain value and make your home ready to place on the market.

But one word of warning: If you're a sloppy painter, especially with the edge work, get a professional to do the job. It will be worth it.

I recently listed a home that had been completely repainted by the owners in neutral gray, but the work was untidy around the ceiling line. When I held my first open house, nearly every prospective buyer noticed the sloppy paint job and commented on it. I reported this complaint back to the sellers, and they corrected it, and the house sold soon thereafter.

Take the time to tape off areas to get the straightest lines possible. Prep work is vital. Usually two coats are necessary on a wall, but the new paints that contain primer make it possible to get away with just one coat.

And by all means, ask your REALTOR® what color to use. You may hate REALTOR® beige, or REALTOR® gray, or REALTOR® coastal blue — but your buyers will love it. To be more specific, your buyers will love that your walls have been neutralized and are no longer a distraction to their ability to see the other great features of the room.

Throw your own tastes out the window and let the buyers visualize

The bright yellow walls were a distraction in this beautiful home, so the owners repainted and neutralized the background. Along with some Staging this allowed buyers to see the other great features of the home. This is also another example of what I discussed in Chapter 2, that RED ROCKS. On the right, the red accents pull your eye around the room and create a sense of space.

---

their own specific tastes in your home. They can only "see" their own style clearly through the clean, neutralized lens of your freshly painted and Staged home.

> **TIP #11: If you can only do one thing to Stage your home, PAINT! It is the best, least expensive way to add value.**

One final painting tip: DO NOT paint your walls white in order to neutralize them. White is viewed as too stark by most buyers. Grays, beiges, light blues and soft greens are now included in the neutral pallette.

Not only are white walls out, but so is the old rule that you can't display personal photos. So go ahead and display them — but be judicious when doing so; limit the personal photos to attractive ones in handsome frames that set the right mood.

Accent walls that are either painted a complementary color, or are accented with tasteful shiplap paneling or wallpaper, are very popular in today's market.

But beware also of fads. What might bring the buyers running this year could repel them next year.

Chapter 8

Home Buyer, Thy Name is Woman

Years ago I got the goofy idea to paint stencils on the risers of my steps leading to the second story. This was the 1980s and stenciling was the "in" thing, so I really went to town and stenciled little colorful baskets of flowers on the risers. I cringe now to think of it, but it was very cute back then.

Eventually I had to sell the house, but I couldn't bear to paint over my stencils, so I just left them on the steps and hoped for the best.

I was just grabbing my purse to run out the front door one morning when a couple came in with their REALTOR® to view my home. The

first thing they saw was my stenciling on the steps. Clasping her hands together, the wife gushed: "Oh, I LOVE the steps!" That very day I received an offer from them.

I relate this story NOT to convince you to paint stencils all over your house, please don't — but to explain how emotional buyers can be when buying a home. Are cheesy stencils any reason to buy a house? Of course not, but in my rare case they helped cinch the deal by creating a special feeling in the heart of that young woman.

Woman are the key decision-makers more than 95 percent of the time in buying, and even renting, a home.

My personal experience is that women react to a home much more emotionally than men. Before anyone gets offended by this statement and calls it sexist, it is NOT a bad thing. Women can "feel" themselves living in a particular home, whereas men are often more analytical, examining heating systems, electrical boxes and attic insulation and overlooking awkward floor plans and out-of-date kitchens that women can zero in on with laser-like precision.

Ultimately both men and women need to "feel" they can live in the home they are viewing, but always keep in mind that your Home Staging needs to create an emotional hook for the women first, and then stand back and let the gals convince the guys.

A 2015 study conducted by the online property portal *Housing.com* confirms that my personal experiences are not unusual. The study found that woman are the key decision makers more than 95 percent of the time in buying, and even renting, a home.

Women aged 18 to 34 are the most active in real estate decisions. And nearly 60 percent of the users on *Housing.com* are women.

The influential role of emotion in consumer behavior is well documented. Neuro-imagery shows that when evaluating brands, consumers (both men and women) primarily use their personal feelings and experiences rather than information to make a buying decision.

Research conducted by the Advertising Research Foundation concluded that the emotions of "likeability" are the measure most predictive of whether an advertisement will increase a brand's sales. So if you can appeal to the woman's emotional response to "likeability," you may nail the sale.

> **TIP #12: Stage your home to appeal to women. The men will follow.**

Staging your home to appeal to women does NOT mean you should overdo it on the frills, the color pink, the gingham and lace. Anything but. A home that is too frilly, too girly, or too "granny," is a turn-off. But nothing is a bigger turnoff to a woman's sensibility than a home that is uber-masculine, like the camo-festooned home described in Chapter 2.

Several years ago I Staged a home owned by a lovely young couple who were moving out of the state. Their home was as neat as a pin, with the kind of minimalist style that is a Stager's dream. As I walked through the home I thought it would require almost no decluttering and Staging — until I entered the man cave. I could almost smell the testosterone!

Looking around that cluttered man cave I saw a bicycle hanging from the ceiling, a bookcase lined with a baseball cap collection and beer cans, Harley Davidson memorabilia, a baseball and mitt enshrined in plexiglass, a gigantic TV screen that filled one entire wall, an oversized leather recliner with dirty frayed pillows, license plates with colorful, and off-color, names on the wall, and a Confederate flag. That was just for starters.

The seller who allows his house to be Staged but keeps the man cave sacrosanct is running a big risk. He is gambling that buyers will love every other room in the house enough to overlook the room he can't bear to touch. It's a bad risk, because EVERY room in the house needs to have a purpose. That man cave should have been Staged as a fourth bedroom, office or den — not a shrine to his Y chromosome, no offense to you men out there.

TIP #13: Never stage a room to look too masculine, or too feminine.

Having the room packed with male-inspired décor was not the only problem with this room. It also violated one of the first rules of Home Staging: Declutter! If this room had nothing in it but the TV, the leather recliner and a couple of colorful pictures on the wall, it might have given off the right vibe for a den. But the masculine overkill was also a killer for any sale.

What finally happened in this room? I reminded the husband that he's moving soon anyway, and that he might as well pack up his precious belongings for the new home now, rather than risk prospective home buyers damaging them.

I convinced the husband, with the wife's cagey assistance, to disassemble the man cave. After much agonized soul-searching on his part, he finally removed most of his collectibles and we Staged the room as a den.

TIP #14: Home owners should securely pack up their belongings now for their next home. This helps avoid clutter overload.

Another homeowner I met had gone to the other extreme. This young single woman was as cute as a Barbie doll, and her home was as pink and ruffled as a Barbie dream house. There were stuffed animals on every bed, walls were painted every possible shade of pink, and nearly every nicknack in the house was pink and covered in ruffles.

The first thing she said to me was, "Yeah, I know it's kind of a girly house. What do I need to do to get it looking right for buyers?"

This young lady got it! I knew she would be a breeze to work with!

Chapter 9
Grab Them at the Curb

When my husband and I were married, our first decision was, which house should we sell, and which house should we live in. It was actually quite a dilemma, because both houses had pros and cons, but in the end we decided to stay in my house and sell his.

First, however, the house had to be spruced up from top to bottom and Staged.

It was easy to fix up the inside. We refinished the hardwood floors, and put in new kitchen cabinets and countertops. The entire inside was painted, bathrooms were updated, and then the house was Staged. It looked fabulous!

But outside was another story. Although it had new windows, a new roof and new vinyl siding, it was still pretty blah. It needed some landscaping and some additional appeal.

The appeal took the form of new landscaping, painting the rough spots, adding shutters, and we used red mulch for a pop of additional color. Fresh mulch of any color works wonders for tired-looking flower beds.

Landscaping does not always come cheap. But the money spent on landscaping can make the difference between a fast sale and a home that languishes on the market.

I listed a new home a few years ago in a subdivision where all the homes were brand new. This home was a pretty cape cod (see next page) with a rocking-chair front porch situated on the cul-de-sac. It should have sold quickly — but the builder neglected to add any landscaping. It sat on the market for months and sold well below its asking price because of this one drawback.

This home languished on the market for months and eventually sold well below its asking price because it lacked curb appeal. On the right, landscaping (Photoshopped in through Virtual Staging, see next chapter) clearly makes this home more appealing to buyers.

On MANY occasions I have brought buyers to a home, but they have declined to go inside based purely on the lack of curb appeal. Buyers may understand that the only thing lacking is some landscaping and a more welcoming look, but they can't "feel" that the home could possibly be theirs without curb appeal.

That *feeling* is what sells the house!

How to Add Curb Appeal:

- Give your front door a makeover. At a minimum, paint your door. You can also add a pretty door knocker or house number.

- Add outdoor lighting. Landscape lighting makes a huge impact on your home's curb appeal and also provides security. You can also add accent lighting to trees or the house, or you can illuminate a walking path. You can also go the easy route by installing solar light fixtures.

- Create the look of a flower garden by using container flowers. Container gardens add color and a welcoming feel to any home exterior quickly, easily and affordably. You can buy ready-made containers from garden centers or create your own.

The front of this house was blah, so we painted the porch and trim white, painted the steps, added shutters, added some shrubs and plants, and laid down red mulch for color. The end result was a quick sale with multiple offers!

- Do a mailbox makeover. Mailboxes should complement the home. Dress up mailboxes for curb appeal by painting the wooden post to match the house's exterior color, or by surrounding it by a beautiful flowering garden.

- Add shutters or accent trim. Shutters and trim add another layer of personality and curb appeal. Exterior shutters can be inexpensively purchased at home-improvement stores and you can mount them yourself.

- Renew paint, siding and trim. An exterior facelift (new paint, siding or trim details) automatically transforms the look of a home. Any obvious defects, such as cracked siding or loose bricks, can turn away home buyers and should be repaired.

- Tile your doorstep, porch or walkway — or all of these areas. This creates a permanent welcome mat and adds value in the eyes of buyers.

- Declutter the front yard of lawn ornaments, statues, bird baths, bird houses, and anything else that may detract from its appeal.

TIP #15: Don't neglect the importance of curb appeal.

Chapter 10
No Vacancy

What do you do when you have a vacant home to sell?

This can occur when a family has found a new home and needs to move out before their old home has sold ... or when new construction is completed and ready to sell ... or often when family members inherit a property from parents and need to sell it. The scenarios that trigger vacant homes are endless.

The answer is that you still need to Stage your vacant home — but you will be bringing everything you need INTO the home instead of removing items.

There is nothing more boring than looking at photos online of barren rooms, four walls, a window or two and a door. Most buyers can't imagine the size of the room without seeing some furniture in it for scale, and they won't have any idea how to live in that room with their own furnishings if it is not Staged.

There are several ways to Stage a vacant home if you don't have the furnishings you need already in place:

Rent or Borrow Furniture

Years ago when my husband and I were selling his home I knew we needed to Stage it. I wasn't even a Home Stager back then, but instinctively I knew it needed some furniture.

We had revamped the kitchen entirely, painted the whole house inside, refinished the hardwood floors, perked up the exterior with some new landscaping ... but still it look bare and cold inside.

So I cajoled my husband into loading up his truck with some of my own furniture and tchotchkes and I Staged the living room, dining room, kitchen and master bedroom. Then I scheduled an open house and soon the offers (yes, multiple) began to pour in.

The house was great as it was, but the Staging made it fabulous. The buyers who visited the open house could feel themselves living there only because it was Staged.

TIP #16: Stage your vacant home or your vacant rooms.

What I had done was borrow Staging items from myself — but renting furniture is another great option. The only downside to rentals is that if your home sits on the market too long the rental fees could add up.

Most Home Stagers (myself included) have all the Staging items that sellers will need, including dining room tables, coffee tables and living room layouts.

My Staging Partner, Judy Woten, and I have closets full of our Staging items collected after nearly a decade of Staging. We can accommodate nearly every color scheme and style with our stash of Staging paraphernalia.

This living room was completely devoid of furniture, except for a plastic lawn chair. With no access to a sofa, our Staging team used two dining room chairs and a table to create the illusion of a sitting area. The home got under contract in less than a week.

VirtuallyStagedRealEstate.com is one of many virtual Staging services available. This is one of their virtually Staged rooms, which shows the vacant room and then the digitally enhanced Staged room on the right. This type of Staging looks so appealing and realistic that it is a great alternative to actual Staging — but always make sure it is allowed by your Multiple Listing Service.

Virtual Staging

Another emerging trend is "Virtual Staging." This involves taking pictures of vacant rooms, and then digitally inserting furnishings and nick-nacks to show how the room can look when lived in.

There is a danger to this method, however. Virtual Staging is tricking the viewer into seeing a room that doesn't actually exist. In some real estate markets it is a violation of the Multiple Listing Service rules to mislead or doctor photos, so this method should be used with caution.

How to Stage Vacant Rooms

Remember TIP #2, which states that all Staging should be done with the photos in mind. Rooms don't have to be crammed with furniture to look like a livable room. Remember that you're trying to give the buyer only the impression of living space.

- If you don't have an extra sofa, try putting two dining room chairs together in front of the fireplace to mimic a living room seating area.

- To make a bed where there isn't one, create a fake bed out of boxes. We have created so many of these boxes, which we usually top with an air mattress, that almost no one knows they're fake. More than once buyers have attempted to sit on our cardboard beds and ended up sprawled on the floor in the middle of a pile of boxes.

- To Stage an office in a vacant room, use a small credenza or table, add a chair, then put a notepad or laptop computer on it and you've got an instant office.

Both of these beds were created in vacant rooms using boxes topped with air mattresses. They provide enough context in the rooms to show where beds and furniture can be placed once a buyer moves in. Buyers don't even notice that we havent included dressers; what they notice is the spaciousness of the rooms.

Our Staging team has rooms filled with Staging items, collected over more than a decade of Staging homes in the Lynchburg, Virginia, region.

Chapter 11
I Did WHAT?

I recently received a glowing review from a satisfied seller whose home I had Staged and gotten under contract in just four days. Needless to say, this couple was thrilled with my service.

The review read, in part:

> *Patti spent about a month with us before selling our home. She went through our whole house and told us what to do with each piece. She also told us to replace the dishwasher, stove, and refrigerator. She contacted Sears and arranged for them to remove ours and install theirs. She provided cleaners and utility workers to do several needed repairs ... Patti and her whole office came to our house and, using our furniture and many of her special added effects, she Staged our home to make each room appear to have more square feet.*

> *Patti advertised our home on the internet on Thursday for an open house on Saturday and Sunday. We had eight families visit both days. Five different families gave us an offer. Patti helped us communicate with each one and gave us many good ideas on how to get the final offer approved. Patti also represented us all the way to closing. Patti deserves a five-star rating as the best possible agent anyone could ever want to use.*

Wow! It exhausted me just to read all that I had done. Did I really do all that just to get that house to sell? The answer is YES ... and I did much more. I shopped at several bath stores to find exactly the right shower curtain to match the tiles in the master bathroom. I polished the countertops and sinks prior to the open house to make them gleam. I swept the rear deck of leaves. I picked up leaves and debris by hand from the landscaping in the front of the house. On

This cluttered kitchen needed much more than just decluttering. The homeowner agreed to new vinyl flooring, countertops, cabinets and paint, and the result (right) was dramatic. This home sold in just days with multiple offers.

open house day I cleaned the tiles by the back door. And I changed lightbulbs that were too dim to properly show off the property.

The point is this: Staging a home is not a simple matter of decluttering, rearranging furniture and matching colors. Staging is one item in the toolbox that sells a home. A Staged home looks a lot better with freshly painted walls, new appliances, updated light fixtures, and new granite countertops. All these tool in the toolbox, along with Staging, help sell the home.

The very first thing I do, once I have landed a listing, is to walk through the house with the homeowners and give them a "to-do" list. In the case of the sellers above, I recommended new kitchen countertops along with the appliances, but the expense turned out to be more than the homeowners wanted to bear. So although the countertops from the 1970s remained in the kitchen, we scrubbed and polished them and paired them with brand-new stainless steel appliances. Without exception, the kitchen was the highlight of the house because of the new appliances.

TIP #17: Don't lose sight of the bigger picture. If the house has outdated features, try to get your homeowners to make some upgrades, then Stage it.

As my Home Staging business progresses, I have made numerous contacts along the way who I can bring on a job quickly. One of my best contacts is the Sears salesman. He gives me discounted prices on all the appliances my clients need, and I give him a lot of business in return.

Rich, one of my favorite lenders, can pre-qualify a client quickly. And when he pre-qualifies them it's nearly guaranteed they will get the loan. My painters will drop everything to paint a few rooms for me. And my handyman can handle nearly every small and medium job I need tackled.

Cultivating good relationships with such professionals goes hand in hand with Home Staging … and it makes you, the real estate agent, look like a seasoned orchestra leader keeping all the different players working in harmony.

One of my recent listings posed additional challenges, and during the grueling course of the listing, Staging and sale I learned a valuable new lesson: Learn when to say no.

The seller was the biggest problem. At the outset of the listing he announced he was moving out of the house into a nursing home, and so he did — but after he moved out he left me with a dirty house filled with junk, and no family members to help clear out the mess. So I rolled up my sleeves and I hired a cleaning crew, Staged the property, and got it on the market. It was at least a week of daily packing, moving furniture into the garage and cleaning to get the property show ready, but ready it eventually was — and it got Staged and listed.

Unfortunately, the seller liked to come back for occasional visits, and when he did he left the home an untidy mess for me to straighten up over and over again. Finally, on one of my unannounced visits to the house to make sure all was well, I walked in and found the seller lying on the floor unable to get up. He had

> "Help, I've fallen and I can't get up ... call my Realtor!"

fallen during the preceding night, injured his hip, and could not get up.

I called an ambulance and he was taken to the hospital to convalesce. In the meantime, you guessed it, I had to clean up the house yet again. He ultimately ended up in another nursing home, and there he blessedly stayed until he was recovered ... and his home had sold.

The lesson for me was profound: I am ultimately the REALTOR® and Home Stager, not the caretaker, psychologist or maid. I will go above and beyond, but there must be a limit to the "beyond." I will say "no" in the future if I see the signs of a seller who is shaping up to be that difficult.

And my advice for homeowners is this: Let your REALTOR® and other professionals do their jobs without throwing roadblocks in their way.

CONCLUSION

Despite all the adventures — or in some cases, misadventures — I have described in this book, I LOVE being a Home Stager. The reasons should be obvious:

Home Staging sells homes, and it sells homes faster and for more money than unstaged homes!

What's more, the transformation of a typical home into a Staged home is a profound one. I can't count the number of times home owners have waivered in their commitment to selling after seeing how beautiful their homes look after Home Staging.

We have Staged homes ranging from "soft Staging," which involves using the home owners' furnishings and decorations and just de-cluttering and tweaking — to full glamour Staging, in which we bring in furniture and accent pieces, and essentially "design" the house to sell from the floor up.

Here are a few final tips:

> **TIP #18: Modern design elements are more attractive to buyers than old-fashioned, ornate furnishings. Modernize your look to attract buyers.**

Today's buyers can "see" their own style more clearly through the clean lines of modern furnishings than they can through an ornate, old-fashioned design.

Most buyers today fit into the millennial category. The median age of first-time buyers is 32, according to the National Association of REALTORS®. This explains why today's buyers know what the trends are, and they know what they want. They are the buyers that home sellers need to cater to.

> **TIP #19: Homeowner, don't take Staging advice personally. Your REALTOR®/Home Stager is not making judgements about your taste when she recommends changes.**

As Michael Corleone says in "The Godfather" ... "It's not personal, it's strictly business." Of course, he was referring to wacking a couple of his rivals, but you get the general idea.

Home Staging is a marketing tactic, it's a business decision — and home owners should understand this. Even Home Stagers go home at night and flop down in their untidy homes with their friendly clutter about them and don't think twice about the fact that their homes need Staging (except, of course, my Staging partner, Judy, who we've already established lives in a perpetually Staged home).

"It's not personal, Sonny, it's strictly business."

My final advice to home owners thinking of selling is this: Do your homework. Research home sales in your neighborhood. Understand what sells, for how much, and how fast.

And once you have all the facts, understand that buyers have the same information — because it's readily available on the Internet. Today's buyers are the most savvy ones I've ever seen because they sometimes troll the web for a year or more before finally calling a REALTOR® to view a home.

So to get ahead of the competition in your market, price your home right ... and Stage It!

> **TIP #20: Do your research before you list, and if you can't find the information call your REALTOR® to do it for you. Then price your home right and Stage it!**

SUMMARY OF TIPS

TIP #1: Use color strategically to draw the eye around a room and away from features you don't want to highlight.

TIP #2: ALWAYS consider how the room you are Staging will look in a photo. If the red valence you're placing on the window is drawing the eye to a broken window pane, rethink the valence.

TIP #3: Declutter every room, closet and space in your house by removing items that don't enhance its appeal.

TIP #4: Leave the corners of rooms as open as possible to create the impression of more space.

TIP #5: Neutralize strong themes in rooms to appeal to the largest number of buyers.

TIP #6: Be respectful of sellers' belongings, and of their strong connection to their home's decor.

TIP #7: You're not selling your home; you're selling square footage.

TIP #8: Most buyers need to be shown the room's purpose. Show buyers how to use the room by Staging it.

TIP #9: There is no substitute for a clean house. Clean sells!

TIP #10: Eliminate all odors from the house with a thorough house cleaning. Don't try to mask strong odors with a lot of plug-ins, perfumes or candles.

TIP #11: If you can only do one thing to Stage your home, PAINT! It is the best, least expensive way to add value.

TIP #12: Stage your home to appeal to women, without being overly feminine. The men will follow.

TIP #13: Never Stage a room to look too masculine, or too feminine.

TIP #14: Home owners should securely pack up their belongings now for their next home. This helps avoid clutter overload.

TIP #15: Don't neglect the importance of curb appeal.

TIP #16: Stage your vacant home or your vacant rooms.

TIP #17: Don't lose sight of the bigger picture. If the house has outdated features, try to get your homeowners to make some upgrades, then Stage it.

TIP #18: Modern design elements are more attractive to buyers than old-fashioned, ornate furnishings. Modernize your look to attract buyers.

TIP #19: Homeowner, don't take the Staging advice personally. Your REALTOR®/Home Stager is not making judgements about your taste when she recommends changes.

TIP #20: Do your research before you list, and if you can't find the information call your REALTOR® to do it for you. Then price your home right and Stage it!

ACKNOWLEDGEMENTS

Many thanks to Judy Woten, my Staging partner and Broker, for her helpful suggestions with this book, and her longtime guidance in my real estate career, and her friendship.

Most of the photographs in this book were taken by my colleague at The Real Estate Advantage, Steve Burkett. Thank you, Steve, for your photography and Staging assistance through the years.

I am so grateful to my many clients over the years who have allowed me to come into their homes and unleash the tornado that is our Staging team. I know that the process of Staging can be disruptive and uncomfortable, yet my clients have shown incredible patience and cooperation with me and my Staging team — and for that I am truly thankful.

Patti Pierucci

Made in the USA
Middletown, DE
06 December 2017